KV-203-437

Living in a One-Sided House

PUDNEY, J.

COMHLEABHARLANNA CHONTAE THIOBRAD ARANN

(County Tipperary Joint Libraries)

ACC. No. K 7235 CLASS No 821/PUD

Date of Return	Date of Return	Date of Return

PUDNEY. J.
LIVING IN A ONE-SIDED HOUSE.

821 PUD/K.7235   DONATION BY WM.
                 ENGLISH.

LIVING IN A
ONE-SIDED HOUSE

Poems by
JOHN PUDNEY

for reading for fun
for saying out loud
for joining in
for acting out on tape

COUNTY TIPPERARY JOINT LIBRARIES
County Library
Thurles

SHEPHEARD-WALWYN
LONDON

First published 1976 by Shepheard–Walwyn
(Publishers) Limited, London.

Certain poems have appeared in Ambit, Country
Life, Cricket (USA), The New Statesman and Nova,
on B.B.C. radio and television and on ITV.

© Poems: John Pudney 1976
© Illustrations: Shepheard–Walwyn (Publishers) Limited 1976

All rights reserved

No part of this publication may be reproduced, stored
in a retrival system, or transmitted in any form
or by any means, electronic, mechanical, photocopying,
recording or otherwise, without prior permission
of Shepheard–Walwyn (Publishers) Limited.

ISBN 0 85683 032 1

COUNTY TIPPERARY
Joint Libraries Committee

Acc. No. K 7235

Class No. 821/PUD

Pres. Donation
William English

Vendor Clonmel

Catalogued CR.

Printed in Great Britain by
Unwin Brothers Limited
Old Woking, Surrey

Contents

LIVING IN A ONE-SIDED HOUSE

The people who live in the one-sided house
Say it's only a matter of learning the knack
Of living without two sides or a back.

They answer the door to tell you this
But they don't ask you in
Unless you are quite exceptionally thin.

"The advantage, we claim,
For a house of this kind
Is
You don't have the back or two sides
On your mind.
When out,
This is less of a worry, we find."

COUNTY TIPPERARY JOINT LIBRARIES
County Library
Thurles

THE PINK RABBIT

"In the van in the Park
There's a man seven feet high
Designing a waterfall," said the rabbit.

That pink rabbit is such a liar that I
Gave a take-you-with-a-pinch-of-salt kind of sigh:
"A waterfall?"

"Yes," said the rabbit,
"But perhaps he's only six feet."
That rabbit is the biggest liar
On four or even two legs I think.

"Six feet tall? Designing a waterfall?
Rabbit," I said, "I like you because you're pink,
But when you talk about men
Designing waterfalls . . . I have doubts then."

"Only one man," said the rabbit,
"And perhaps only five feet ten.
I only exaggerate
Because the idea of a waterfall is so great,
A work of art!"

"You've dreamt it, that part,
But I'll believe the part about the man
Being five feet ten. . . ."

"I'm five foot ten and a bit!"
Snorted the Park Superintendent,
Getting out of his van.
"And it's a silly habit,
Talking to yourself." He glared at me.

"But, Superintendent, you didn't notice a rabbit?
A pink rabbit you didn't happen to see?"

"Nothing like that," he glared.
"Nothing like that at all.
I'm too busy. Look at this
Design I'm making for a waterfall."

OUR HERO

The man who had mended the Queen's refrigerator
Came to live in our street
And you might have thought
(From the curiosity) he was a man
Who had crossed the Sahara Desert
In bare feet.

Though there was nothing but a bit of moustache
Clinging to this man's face
You might have thought
(For the interest, that is) he had just come back
From fixing things
On the moon or in outer space.

Everyone knew that he
Must have *opened* the Queen's refrigerator

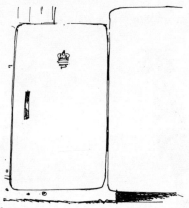

To mend it,
Then tested it, tried it,
Before shutting it again;
And everyone was waiting, in vain,
For the man to say what had been inside it.
"Peacock pie or passion fruit flan
Or sturgeon steaks?" they would ask the man.

Then the man would look very
Sincere though matter-of-fact
And say "I always oblige when I can:
But even to hint at what I saw or didn't see
Would break the Official Secrets Act.
And that would be the end
Of a refrigerator mender like me."

So the man who had mended the Queen's refrigerator
Was a hero to us: and to his Queen not a traitor.

THE FISH WHO TURNED HIS BACK

The fish in the aquarium
Who turned his back on the audience
Said, frowning,
"I don't like to see the people out there drowning."

THE EARL OF SLOUGH

The Earl of Slough
Has had enough.
"I rhyme with 'bough'
And not with 'rough'.

"Please tell me how
To let them know
In the town of Slough
That I rhyme so:—
Though I bend a bow
I take a bow.
Though with corn I sow,
My pig is a sow."

The Earl of Slough
With a nervous cough
Says "That's all now,
I must be off."

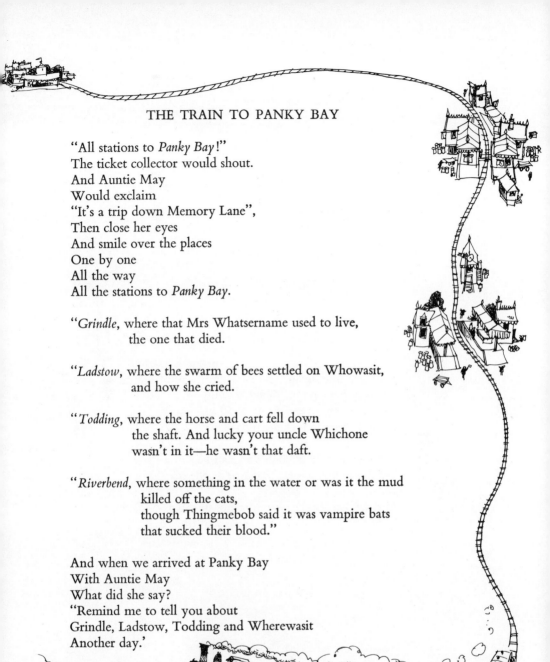

THE TRAIN TO PANKY BAY

"All stations to *Panky Bay*!"
The ticket collector would shout.
And Auntie May
Would exclaim
"It's a trip down Memory Lane",
Then close her eyes
And smile over the places
One by one
All the way
All the stations to *Panky Bay*.

"*Grindle*, where that Mrs Whatsername used to live,
        the one that died.

"*Ladstow*, where the swarm of bees settled on Whowasit,
        and how she cried.

"*Todding*, where the horse and cart fell down
        the shaft. And lucky your uncle Whichone
        wasn't in it—he wasn't that daft.

"*Riverbend*, where something in the water or was it the mud
        killed off the cats,
        though Thingmebob said it was vampire bats
        that sucked their blood."

And when we arrived at Panky Bay
With Auntie May
What did she say?
"Remind me to tell you about
Grindle, Ladstow, Todding and Wherewasit
Another day.'

THE PIANO TUNERS

They are fine piano tuners but creatures of whim.
Nobody ever taught them to swim:
And by some oversight or mischance
Nobody ever taught them to dance.

So you see how difficult they can be,
Whimsically wanting to dance on the sea.

And who will tune all the pianos in town
If they trip up, trying to dance, and drown?

THE BOLD SHIP'S COOK

He trembled at the tread of toads,
He cowered at cows
And hid from bees.
He wouldn't go through woods
For fear of animals in trees.
And yet he made a bold ship's cook
And sailed the seven seas.

The first sea snarled and spat at him,
The second raged,
The third one rolled.
The fourth sea blistered him,
The fifth turned his blood cold,
The sixth was blind with fog,
The seventh boiled.
He went on being bold.

A bolder cook no ship could wish.
His boldness spread
With every tide.
He boldly stirred his pots,
He boldly grilled and fried.
Until a mouse who joined the ship,
Hungry and lost and beady-eyed,
Peeped at him round the galley door:
Which so alarmed him that he died.

DOG BUSINESS

Old Dog, on dog business intent,
Padding from smell to scent,
Sniffing snuffing he goes,
Following his nose.

Dog conversations with friends are bluff,
Hearty and gruff,
Long sniff short snuff,
And, *politesse* without fail,
A ceremonial flourish of the tail.

Dog business, of course, may include
Enemies to be confronted:
When hackles rise, bared teeth obtrude.
Times also when fragrant objects
Or creatures that elude
Need to be hunted,
Though not exhaustively pursued.

Old Dog is not without reproductive itch
And dog business may entail
A sentimental trail
In company canine and female
With somebody's cherished bitch.

No good whistling Old Dog then,
Or calling his name
With soft persuasive tone.
Though he loves his own
People just the same,

He, on dog business, chooses to be alone;
Pursuing love or, more important,
Burying his bone.

Old Dog on dog business intent.
Watch him purposefully roam,
Following his nose from smell to scent,
Yet always, at the finish
of dog business,
Coming home.

HOW TO STOP A GRASSHOPPER HOPPING

You can't stop a grasshopper hopping
Unless you say: *Please*
Tell us which are your ELBOWS
And which are your KNEES?

Sometimes then the grasshoppers will stop hopping
And say: *We hate stopping*
For people who raise silly points.
We call them JOINTS.

 THE BAMBALOO

The brand new birds that came from above
Knew each other as Phyllis and James,
Or Phil and Jim when they said it with love.
They never thought about PROPER names.

But people on earth like to register things
Both aeroplanes and birds with wings;
"If not you're *unidentified*"
The brand new birds were told. "And then
People chase after you far and wide
To find out which is the cock and the hen.
They goggle at you with binoculars
And examine you, top to tail, from afar.
They search for your nest with choppers and cars.
They may kill you to find out who you are."

But how to sign on as birds brand new?
When Jim and Phil sought advice on names
No bird they encountered had much of a clue—
Except that being called Phyllis and James,
Even Jim or Phil, wouldn't do.

An elderly pigeon said "Try a Zoo."
So they preened and cleaned themselves and flew
To the nearest one and prepared to land
Where all kinds of birds were being polite
And listening to a military band.
Crowds of people, left and right,
Stared and read out their proper names,
Their origins, sometimes their ages.
"I don't like the look of this," said James
"And we can't fly in. They're all in cages."

A Natural History Museum they tried.
"They catalogue everything. They'll be so glad"
Said the pigeon, "of something brand new from outside,
Something they've not already had."
Phil and Jim found a window wide,
Flew in but soon were shocked and sad,
For everything cataglogued had died.
People frowned at them and they felt rebuffed,
For all the birds in there were stuffed.

Though rather scared of such very long words
as ORN-I-THO-LOG-ICAL H.Q.
They bravely announced they were brand new birds,
But were told "You ought to have cards with you,
Stamped with place of origin, date of birth
And time of arrival here on earth."
Phil, who was nesting, cried and cried.
"Our chicks will be unidentified."

Now a garden hedge was their nesting place,
Just the right height and draught-proof and stable
With quite a nice view and a lady called Grace
Who laid out meals on a little bird table.
"My husband's a Poet. He likes to see
Beautiful creatures come and go.
Eat up! If you have some anxiety,
Sing us your troubles sweet and low."

Sweet and low they sang of the shame
Of living without a PROPER name.
The Poet cried "Stop! Stop! My dears!
I've kept a name by me for years and years
On my notion shelf, with spare rhymes and things.
I think we shall find it just the right word,
A word that goes with your beautiful wings.
You can call yourself a BAMBALOO BIRD!"

"Bambaloo! Bambaloo! Bambaloo!" they cried.

19

"Tell people on earth we're identified!"
And they sang brand new songs to Grace and her Poet.
"Bambaloo! Bambaloo! Let everyone know it!"

THE TERRIBLE COST OF SEEING IN THE DARK

The Bambaloo birds can see in the dark.
They boast of not sleeping but seeing at night.
But at night they see everything upside down.
Which prevents them night-walking upright.

To walk about nightly, head between heels
Costs too much effort each Bambaloo feels.
For, you see, they have to walk backwards too,
Which a Bambaloo can rarely do.
So,
As going to sleep is more cosy and cheap,
The Bambaloos, like the rest of us, sleep.

THE HARP

The Harp
At the cupboard door cried
I'm a harp."

And I said: "What?"

"The old lady who played me died.
Saying *what* is silly. Now why
Don't you try?"

"I play chess," I said.
"I'm sorry she's dead."

"But you also play hide-and-seek"
Cried the Harp. "That's how you found me
After nine years, four months, one week
In a cupboard."

"You kept count, did you?"

"Nothing better to do" sighed the Harp.
"But now I wish to be played.
Are you afraid
Of playing harp music or what?"

"Saying *what* is silly," I said.
"I play tennis when the weather is hot.
In winter I play patience for hours,
And hide-and-seek sometimes
At the end of a week.
To play anything else
Would be quite beyond my powers."

"I'm sorry for you," the Harp replied.
"The old lady also said it was quite
Beyond her powers
Before she died.
O what, what, what?
Have I waited for
Nine years, four months and one week
In a cupboard all in vain?"

Slam went the door:
And I could never find the cupboard again.

UNDER THE SEA

Husty, Kusty and Faunch were keen
On having supper under the sea.
Such nice people! Such a nice group!
If only the sea didn't get in the soup!
"We ought to have met for tea" Faunch said.
"We ought to have met for afternoon tea."

So they all got keen on tea instead.
A lighter meal is as good for such
Nice people when you're under the sea . . .
But alas the sea got into the tea.
Faunch said "It doesn't matter much.
Let's make it breakfast instead of tea."

So Kusty laid out breakfast rolls
And marmalade and strawberry jam;
Porridge, of course, and slices of ham.
But the sea got into the porridge bowls.
"There! Breakfast under the sea won't do"
Faunch said. "Try lunch. I leave the choice to you."

Husty and Kusty went up to town
To seek advice from Sam the Clown
On how to manage a midday meal
Under the sea. "I'm a clown not a seal,
And if you're not afraid to drown,
It's simple" said Sam. "Before you begin,
Turn everything carefully upside down.
You'll find the sea will never get in."

So Husty, Kusty and Faunch prepared
An exceptional luncheon under the sea.
It included supper, breakfast and tea.
"That Sam's a wonder" Faunch declared.
"Such clever advice! Such a very wise Clown."
Each porridge bowl, the tea in the cup,

Soup in the plate were turned upside down.
And the sea stayed out as they had their sup
Their lunch, tea, breakfast all in one.
And that was not the end of the fun.
They finished floating bottoms up.

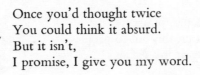

LEFT-HANDED EGG

Before you think twice,
I implore you, I beg,
There's no problem
About a left-handed egg.

Once you'd thought twice
You could think it absurd.
But it isn't,
I promise, I give you my word.

A left-handed egg,
Like a left-handed man,
When frying,
Prefers the left side of a pan.

23

COUNTY TIPPERARY JOINT LIBRARY
County Library
Thurles

THE ORANGE PEACOCK

Please, Mr Gamekeeper!
The Orange Peacock was heard to plead.
All this talk of me as the last of my line,
As I strut round this stately home,
Will make me go into a decline
Long before I need.

If people were to shake their heads at the Earl,
Saying that with an Orange Peacock
And a Verderer and an Estate so vast
What a pity it is that he is the last . . .
He'd have a heart attack.
So they respect his feelings when he struts,
And say it all behind his back.

Now there are no more orange peacocks
Yet there are plenty of earls.
There are, alas, no more orange peahens
But there are plenty of noble girls.
So the Earl can find a mate
Before it is too late,
Instead of leaning loveless over his gilded gate
Or lying alone beneath his painted ceilings.

So, Mr Gamekeeper, please
Couldn't you point this out to people
So that they respect my feelings?

THE PAPER ROSES

When we wanted to buy the paper roses
From the shop window of the optician,
He told us "No. But come back at night.
By day we are all in poor condition,
So bored with testing people's sight.
At night we have roses you don't need to buy.
The roses of all the world fill our night sky.
We dance in the roses' light."

And the man next door said: "He's quite
Quite dotty on his paper roses. We can't think why."

The optician said: "You can come blind
And touch our paper roses
And the fragrance of all the roses in the world
Will dance through your mind.
You can be short- or long-sighted,
Colour-blind or boss-eyed:
The roses of the world will be live and lighted,
The circle of their dance will be high and wide.
This is the paper roses' pride."

And the man next door said:
"In the evenings the optician does get excited
And dances and prances a good deal
When he takes his paper roses inside
And dusts them so that they don't get blighted,
Treating them as if they were real."

THE LADIES

The ladies in the Mercedes
Often irk
Ladies pushing perambulators
Or walking to work.
But the ladies in the Mercedes
Point out
That they give these other ladies
Something to dream about.

HUDDLE

Keep close,
Huddle as close as the snow.
It's one of those days
When the wind blows both ways
(And who can know which way to go?)
When sheep and lions
And tigers and toads
Don't go about,
And keep off the roads.
For the roads go both ways,
Both there and back.
And the wind blows both ways
On every track.

Keep close.
It's a day for holding hands
And staying away
From the far white lands
Where you couldn't tell and wouldn't know
When to come and when to go.

Huddle close
With the lions and tigers
The toads and the sheep.
Hold hands and sleep.

THE LOST NERVE

When Moma made the swerve
   Off the road, on to the municipal flower beds
   And off again
        bomp bomp
         And lost her nerve
   She took the little red scooter bike back
   And put it under the stairs
   Saying
   It wasn't that she'd lost the knack
   Only her nerve;
   It was just the flower beds had taken her unawares
   With their dangerous *bomp bomp* curve.

After that, Moma neglected the red scooter bike.
She might mention it in passing and pat the seat
    (But you've no idea what it is like
    To be a little red scooter bike
    In a dismal dark under-the-stairs retreat)
While Moma never found her nerve
But started going to sleep
In the afternoons as well as at night.
She didn't even speak to the scooter bike to keep
Its spirits up, because the
    bomp bomp bomp
    had given her such a fright.

But the red scooter bike would seize the chance:
As soon as Moma closed her eyes, it would shoot out.
Using a bit of magic which somebody had left about,
It cruised up the street doing a little dance

And anybody who fancied a ride
The red scotter bike urged them to jump on
So all sort of people jumped on and tried
And lost all their cares
And were filled with happiness and pride
Though the scooter bike did feel lonely when they had gone
And it had to creep back under the stairs.

One day Moma ate some magic
          by mistake and felt so good
That in the afternoon she went a walk
Not only around the neighbourhood
To pass the time of day and talk
But down the town hill to visit the sad place,
Where she had lost her nerve that day,
To see if the curve was still a disgrace,
And whether the marks of the *bomp*
          had been tidied away.

By the municipal flower beds she started to cry
And she might have been crying there still
Had not the little red scooter bike chanced to dance by
And, not noticing who the weeping lady was,
          called "Jump on if you'd like a ride up town hill."

"My nerve! It's coming back!" cried Moma as they sped
Up the hill through the town with skill and with verve:
And when they were back without any *bomp* she tenderly said:
"Thank you, dear little scooter bike, for finding my nerve."

CROSS

"The extraordinary thing about footballers,"
Said the cross Man In Green,
"Is that they should always want to be eleven,
DON'T INTERRUPT ME, each side I mean."

I can understand twenty-two playing football.
Good healthy fun
To kick the ball in and out of touch . . . PLEASE
    DON'T MAKE FACES
But couldn't it be done by nine or twenty-one?"

"KINDLY DON'T INTERRUPT ME if I point out
That this is a game
In which always being eleven is ridiculous.
Why should the numbers always be the same?"

"Wouldn't it be much more interesting
If nobody were to know
How many footballers were going to play,
And let this silly notion of eleven go?
What do you say? Eh?"

Crossly the Man In Green said "All I get is INTERRUPTION,
    AND SILLY FACES, just as I feared.
I may as well kick myself into touch!"
And out in the long green grass he disappeared.

GROWING PAINS

I hung out my growing pains to air
To catch the wind and the sun.

"Growing pains? Why there's nothing there!"
My aunts and uncles poked their fun.
"Nothing to see!
        HA HA
           They can't be real!"

How could I explain to everyone
They're not things you see
                but things you feel?

THE BULGARIAN SQUIRREL

"When the Public say *sweety, peety, peaky Bo*!
What kind of English is that?"
The Bulgarian squirrel wants to know.
"They don't know you're Bulgarian, they think
All squirrels in Greenwich Park are English" we say.
"Even when they say *tinky, winky, wink*?"
Asks the Bulgarian squirrel—who had the bad luck
In Bulgaria, by the way,
To fall asleep in a loaded ten-wheeler truck.

It smelt of nuts: and he dreamed of nuts all through
The countries of Europe and over the Channel
Till he woke up on the A2
When the driver stopped on Blackheath
One evening at the public loo.

He wanted to go too.

So he skipped across the road into Greenwich Park
Where the squirrels have little places
      marked LADIES and GENTS,

Though it's difficult to know which is which
      in the dark.
There the Bulgarian squirrel awaited events.

His truck had gone: but he liked the neighbourhood
Where the squirrels live and said he would stay
So long as he could make his language understood:
Which meant that he taught them all Bulgarian there and then,
So that he will always know
What they talk about
        also the difference between WOMEN and MEN.

But when
They try to teach him English
He is slow:
"What does the British Public mean," he will say,
"By *sweety, peety, peaky Bo*?
Are they in pain or is it indigestion?
What am I supposed to think
Of *tinky, winky, wink*?"

And who can answer the Bulgarian squirrel's question?

HIM AND HIS SHIP

I never thought much of his ship.
Though it was so much more of a ship
    than any ship of mine
    than any ship I had sailed in
    than any ship I had dreamed of
I never thought much of his ship

She sailed the seven seas of course his ship
With icebergs
    flying fish
    sperm whales
    the aurora borealis and the albatross
    Midnight Sun
    North Star and Southern Cross
She had ridden through the worst
    and weathered the best his ship

And made me feel like a
Boating lake attendant on a wet Sunday
So I never thought much of his ship

I never thought much of his ship
Until the rain stopped and he stopped too
And water was in his eyes instead
And he cried instead of talking about his ship

34

I suddenly knew then that his ship
Was all in his head
All and only
And that he
Had never been to sea

Then I thought a lot of his ship
      and this I said
It was so much more of a ship
      than any of mine I said

I never thought much of his ship
      until I spoke
      till then
      till he cried
He had seemed just a mean little bloke
Without much of a ship
So I'm glad I said what I did before he died

COUNTY TIPPERARY JOINT
County Library
Thurles

HE THOUGHT HE WAS A MARMALADE CAT

George grew whiskers everywhere:
Out of his ears and down his nose
Up his tummy and over his chest.
"I sometimes think I'm a marmalade cat"
He used to say—of course in jest.

"Perhaps you are a cat in disguise"
Somebody said—in jest of course.
Certainly George had very green eyes.
As he looked at himself in a glass he smirked:
"I'd rather be a cat than a horse
For a cat is rarely overworked
Never has to pull a cart,
Or jump a fence or go on parade.
The life of a cat is a work of art,
A beautiful study in marmalade."

Somebody said—in jest again—
"There's work for a cat in every house.
Not even a marmalade cat would disdain
To hunt an occasional mouse."

"A marmalade cat has a gulp like a king.
A sugar mouse goes down in a trice."
Saying this, George did a terrible thing
He scooped up and swallowed three white mice.

"That's not a joke, They're real! They're real."
Somebody cried. "They're not sugar and spice.
They're Angela's pets. Did you hear them squeal?
The gentleman's swallowed actual mice."

"Though I sometimes think I'm a marmalade cat"
George said "with my whiskers and my very green eyes
I give you my every assurance that
Like the mice I am taken by surprise . . ."

36

Squeals from inside interrupted him:
"Fetch Angela! Help! He's certain to crunch
Or drown us with beer and none of us swim.
He's really a cat and wants us for lunch."

Angela came in floods of tears.
Hearing her pets, she cried
"What have you done to my little dears,
These little white mice in your inside?"

"I thought they were sugar mice" George replied.
"I was having a joke when I swallowed the m down.
I shan't crunch them up. They're safe inside.
I'll keep off the beer so they can't drown."

"Get us out!" cried the mice. "It's too steep to climb.
Angela help! We'll be crunched up or drowned."
"You're giving my pets a most anxious time."
"George! You'd better lie on the ground."

People collected to look at George.
When they heard he'd swallowed three mice they laughed
And crowded around to watch him disgorge.
"He thinks he's a cat" they cried. "He's daft!"

George lay on his back and then on his side.
But the mice hadn't room to move about.
"There's one more method which must be tried.
We'll turn George up and shake them out."

There were cheers when Angela said this.
In no time a tackle and rope were found.
A gentleman upside down! What bliss!
O spread the news around.

"I think it's rather hard on me"
Said George as they all began to haul

Him upside down to the branch of a tree
And Angela called "Open wide and let them fall."

They shook and shook. Then came a shout.
"Stand back you people!" Then came a yell.
The tail of a mouse came slowly out:
Then suddenly out all three mice fell.

Poor George gave a groan. The crowd gave a roar
As they fell. "All safe! Thank goodness for that!"
Angela cried. Then O horror! She saw
The mouth of a real marmalade cat.

This real marmalade cat had sport
As he pounced through the legs of the people bunched
Beneath the tree and skilfully caught
The mice all three, and swallowed and crunched.

WHY I TALK TO THE OWLS

If I talk to the owls on Sydenham Hill
It's surely no surprise.
It's because they're wiser than the owls at Datchet
Who, within reach of London,
Are supposed to be the wisest of the wise.

Now the Druids forgot to take the Sydenham owls
In their wicker baskets when they went west
(Before London was there)
And following the river on their way
Into the sunset
At Datchet they let out the Datchet owls
To take the night air,
But forgot to put them back in the wicker baskets
On the following day
When they went upstream past the oak trees
(Before Windsor was there)
And vanished into the history books, you might say.

But back on Sydenham Hill the owls
A day or so ahead in wisdom,
Had been thinking for themselves without the Druids' aid;
And were also the wiser
For never in wicker baskets having been conveyed.

And this I couldn't have told you about,
And wouldn't myself know it still
Had it not been pointed out,
Casually of course,
By the owls on Sydenham Hill.

PLUS ONE

The milk float Manager counted up,
Drinking tea from a cardboard cup
At the milk float depot beside the sea,
Then called to the milk float Foreman Ben
"How many milk floats make up ten?"

"Why nine plus one, if you ask me."

"I'm asking you if it's really so.
You're a milk float Foreman. You ought to know"
The Manager said to Foreman Ben.
Ben said: "No Manager should ask.
The counting up is the Manager's task.
But nine plus one does make up ten."

And both of them missed a milk float then.

The Manager left the rest of his tea.
Foreman Ben stared out to sea.
"Your sum adds up the same as mine?"
The Manager said: "Not ten but nine?"

"It's the sparkling sea and a touch of the sun,"
Said Ben, "that's lost us that PLUS ONE.
It's the one with the nautical sense of fun.
It's the one that says: *If you call me a float,*
Why shouldn't I go about like a boat?

I'm a float, I'm afloat, I'm afloat! That's me!
Why shouldn't I float on the sparkling sea?
It's a touch of the sun that's hit PLUS ONE."

"But it's loaded up with milk and cream.
It's a nightmare this! A terrible dream!
And butter and eggs!" The Manager cried.
"Our milk float out on the ocean wide!
Suppose it sinks or drifts away
For good? What will our directors say?"

"It may come back on the evening tide,"
Said Foreman Ben, "if we watch and pray."

They watched and prayed throughout the day:
And there on the evening tide was the float,
Empty, bobbing about like a boat.
But the fishermen cried in the setting sun
"What a wonderful thing you've done!
Self-service milk and cream as we fish!
A fully stocked milk float afloat! What fun!
No better service could anyone wish."
The Manager danced to hear them shout
And with Ben cried out "Well done, PLUS ONE."

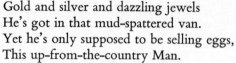

Gold and silver and dazzling jewels
He's got in that mud-spattered van.
Yet he's only supposed to be selling eggs,
This up-from-the-country Man.

    The Egg Man smiles with his eyes at you.
    "Here's eggs," he says, "and a ruby too,
    Red as cherries and love and fire
    To warm you through and through."

    At No. 2 the Egg Man knocks
    And says: "There's an amethyst in the box
    Along with your eggs. It's violet blue
    Like the summer sea and will smile at you."

The Egg Man skips down the garden path
With filigree silver for No. 5.
"Something to go with the eggs," he calls.
"And it's good to be alive!"

One neighbour has a golden crown
Others have sapphire and emerald rings.
Whenever the Egg Man comes to town
The whole street dazzles and sings.

Except for the people at No. 8.
They speak to the Egg Man over their gate.
"We only want *eggs* and we hope they're clean
For your muddy old van isn't fit to be seen."

"You only want eggs?" The Egg Man cries
"You only want eggs?" There are tears in his eyes.
"What else could we want, you silly old man,
Up from the country in that muddy van?"

And so the last of the eggs are sold,
But never the jewels and silver and gold.

THE LITTLE PEOPLE WITH LONG EARS

The problem
Over the little people with long ears
Is that each of them hears what you think.
And if you think their ears are too long
They burst into tears.

So of course you say there's nothing wrong
With the long ears of the little people.
You say they are upright and strong,
Useful for hearing fishermen out at sea,
Or for picking up the distant shout
Of somebody on a hill stung by a bee.

You say this hoping to make them happy again.
But then they hear what you are hoping about
And their tears fall like rain.

THE NOTTERS

All the Not People out on strike!
This is the day I like:
All the Notters stuck indoors,
Not nice
      Not good
            Not mine
                  Not yours.

Stay out on strike, Not People, stay
All day and every other day,
With Not to do
      Not you
            Not much
                  Not to play.

And what do you think they're striking for?
Why, NOTHING I need hardly say.

HEDGEHOGS

I wanted the hedgehogs to make merry
For a merry hedgehog is a fine sight to see.

But the hedgehogs were very very
            edgy about being merry
                    and said to me:

"We hedgehogs might want you to look soppy
For you looking soppy is a fine soppy sight.
But when we say that
            you get sour and acid-droppy
And make out it isn't dignified or very polite."

Perhaps the hedgehogs
(who know a thing or two)
Are right.

CAROL

That first time
Snowflakes didn't fall
There were no jingle bells at all
Father Christmas did not call
There was only love

If there's no lit tree
Down the empty street
For you and me
There's love to eat
With millions more
Like me and you
Behind each door
All making do
With only love
With only love

NOTES

One person can read all or any of the poems silently or out loud and have fun. Or it could be fun to do some of the things I suggest.

Page

NOTES